Fun in America

Sacha de Frisching

Illustrations by Sylvie Rainaud

English edition prepared by Claudia Eilers

Originally published under the title
Les Etats-Unis en salopette by Hachette, Paris.

Photoset by Parker Typesetting Service, Leicester
Printed and bound in France by
Offset Aubin, Poitiers

ISBN 0 330 29235 8

Whilst the advice and information in this book are believed to be true and accurate at the time of going to press, neither the author nor the publisher can accept any legal responsibility or liability for any errors or omissions that may be made

PICCOLO PICTURE BOOKS

Piccolo Globetrotters

USA at a glance

The United States spans an entire continent with as many as 234 million people of every race and colour.

See how the time changes as you cross the country from east to west! Read the clocks to answer our questions.

If it is noon in New York, what time is it in London and in San Francisco?

Solution: It is 5 p.m. in London and 9 a.m. in San Francisco

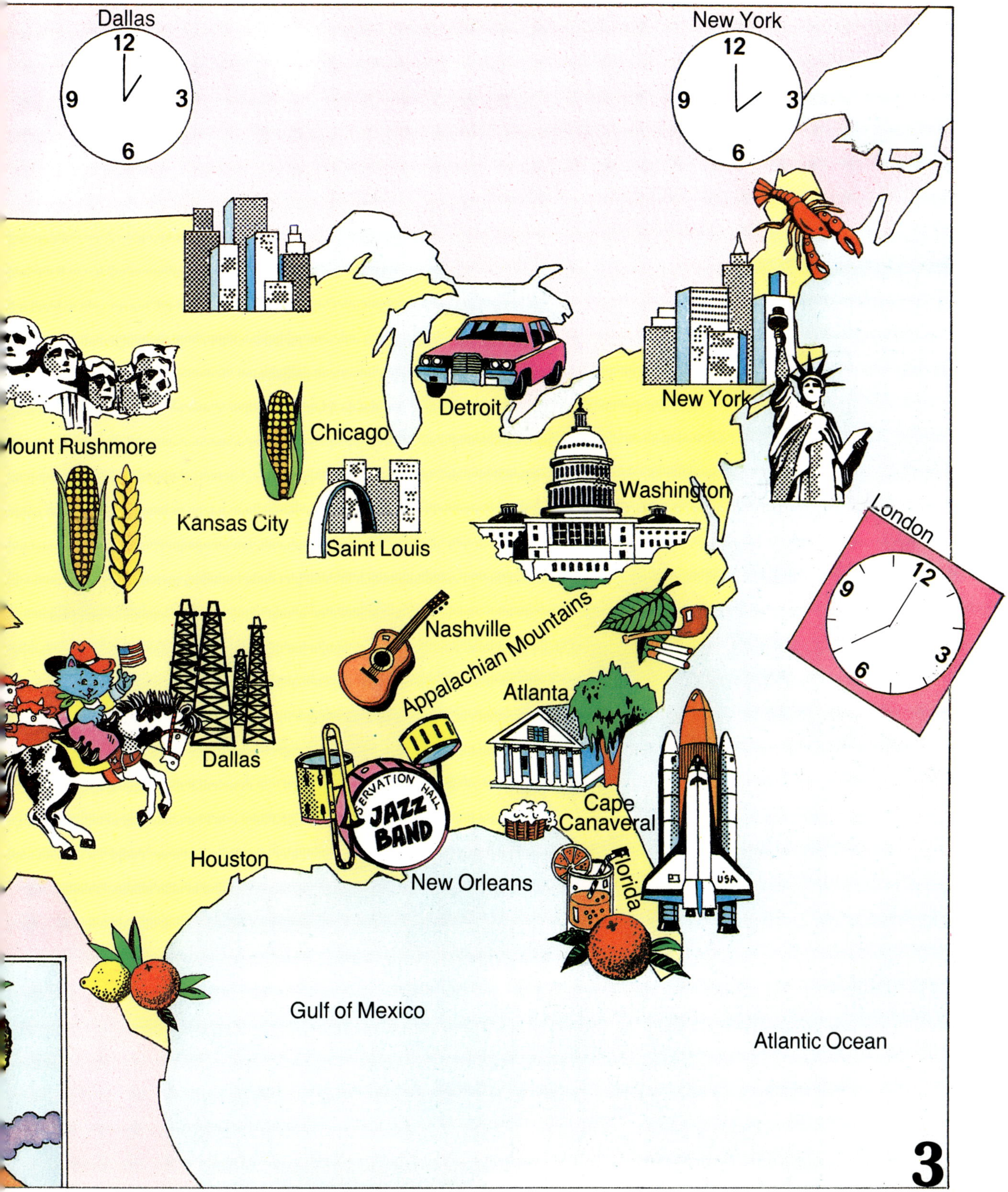
Dallas
12
9
3
6
New York
12
9
3
6
Detroit
New York
Chicago
Mount Rushmore
Washington
London
12
9
3
6
Kansas City
Saint Louis
Nashville
Appalachian Mountains
Atlanta
Dallas
PRESERVATION HALL
JAZZ BAND
Cape Canaveral
USA
Houston
New Orleans
Florida
Gulf of Mexico
Atlantic Ocean

Landscape

The American landscape is incredibly varied, as it stretches from the Arctic Circle to the tropical islands of Hawaii. Look at all these animals and decide where in the wild each of them can be found.

patchwork

Solution: Prairie = prairie-dog, bison, pronghorn. Mountains = grouse, bighorn, grizzly bear. Desert = rattlesnake, coyote. Forest = skunk, chipmunk, squirrel, raccoon. Arctic = polar bear. Swamp = alligator.

American graffiti

The President of the United States
lives in the White House.
Do you know in which city it is?

☐ New York ☑ Washington ☐ Dallas

The Statue of Liberty greets travellers when they arrive at the port of New York. This year it'll be one hundred years old. It was given to the Americans by France.

Now put these monuments in order from the tallest to the smallest and you'll discover the nickname Americans use for New York.

Solution: Washington

Solution: Apple, nickname Big Apple

PELP The big apple = Apple.

Solution: 1 The person on the left is wearing a police badge. 2 The film is coming out of the camera. 3 There is a spanner in the place of the camera handle. 4 The person on the right is using a funnel instead of a megaphone.

America,
In 1620, the Pilgrim Fathers left England on the Mayflower to found the colony of Massachusetts.
The settlers in the South needed workers for their cotton fields and started to bring in slaves from Africa.
On 4th July 1776, the 13 colonies of the New World declared independence for the United States of America.
This started the war of independence which went on for 5 years.
Here are a few milestones from American history. Study the pictures carefully and you'll discover the detail that appears in all of them.

Solution: a star

Stars and Stripes

The Fourth of July
is a national holiday in America.
It marks the anniversary
of the Declaration of Independence
by the colonies on the East coast
which became the first United States.

On the American flag, the stripes stand for the original founder members while the stars indicate the present number of states. Compare the two flags above and find out how many states there were in the beginning and how many there are today.

Trick or treat?

Once a year, on 31st October, the streets are haunted by ghosts and witches who knock on people's doors and offer protection from evil spirits in exchange for a treat. It is Hallowe'en night, and grinning pumpkins light up gardens and windows.

To make your own Hallowe'en lantern simply cut a lid off a pumpkin, hollow it out with a spoon, then cut out the eyes, nose and mouth and put a candlestick inside. After dark, your pumpkin face can glow mysteriously in your bedroom window.

Finger lickin' food!

When the first settlers arrived, the Indians introduced them to plants and animals which did not exist in Europe. Here are a few of them: what are they called and in which dish or product are they used?

Solution: chili = kidney beans; corn on the cob = maize; peanut butter = peanuts; Thanksgiving dinner = turkey; cigarettes = tobacco; pumpkin pie = pumpkin.

Something went wrong here! All the names of these American treats have been jumbled up. You probably know most of them, so put the labels where they belong. Now give each of them your star-rating:

⋆ = good ⋆⋆ = very good ⋆⋆⋆ = extra special

Hit the

Las Vegas is a glittering gamblers' paradise in the desert. Here you'll find fruit machines all over the place: in bars, launderettes, at petrol stations and even in chapels!

jackpot

Try to break the fruit code
by finding the letter for each fruit
and discover the secret message
on each of these one-armed bandits.

Solution: good luck; hello guys; how much; let's go

3.2.1

Lift off!

Journeys into space start at Cape Canaveral. From here Armstrong and Aldrin made their historic trip to the moon.

For the Great Space Race you need four counters and a die. Each player chooses a shuttle to start from. The first to throw a 6 starts the game. You have to go round the board clockwise to get on to the right colour launch pad for the final count-down. The first to reach it wins the race.

Ra! Ra! Ra!

All these sports were invented in the United States. Do you know what they are? Figure out what equipment each of the people in the picture need.

Solution: roller skating, kayak racing, baseball, basketball, football, surfing

Baseball is the national sport.
It is played on a diamond-shaped pitch.
Each team has 9 players
who all play in turn.
The pitcher throws the ball 3 times.
The batsman has to hit it
as far as possible and try to run
right round the pitch before the
other team gets it back to base.

On the road . . .

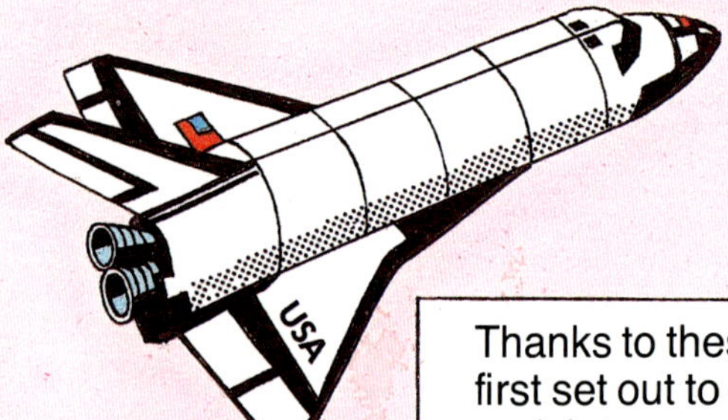

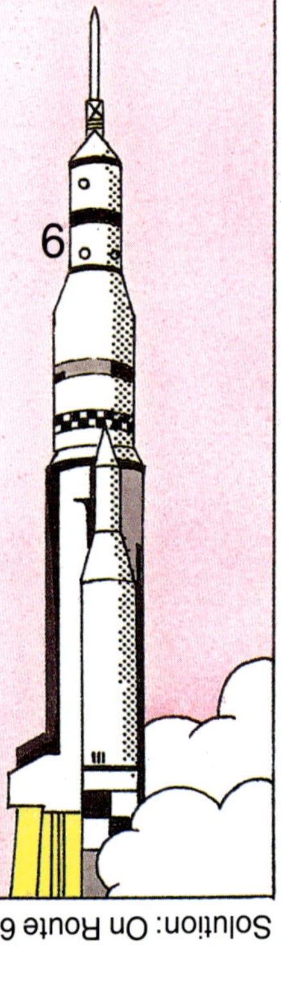

Thanks to these vehicles the Americans first set out to conquer their land and, later on, space.

Try putting them in chronological order: which is the oldest and which the newest? The letters will tell you how to go west.

Solution: On Route 66

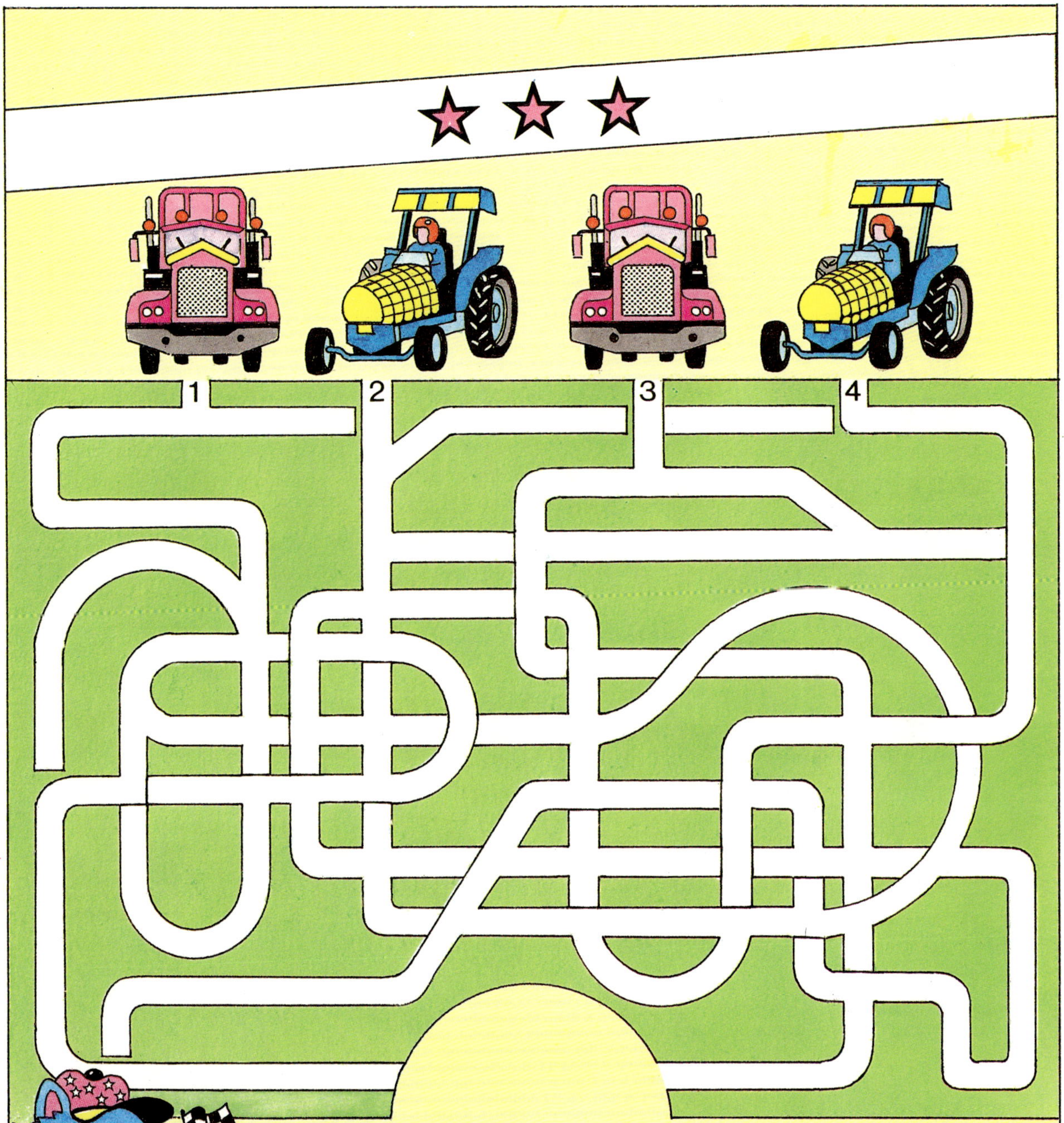

America is the land of big cars,
endless highways, and the most unusual
races for anything on wheels:
trucks, tractors and dragsters –
their crazy custom-built cars.

Who is going to win this race?

Number 3!

Solution: number 3

Cowboys and Indians

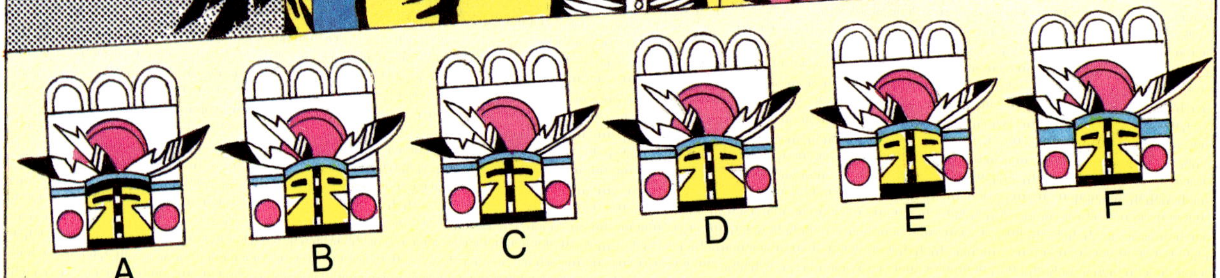

The Indians were the original inhabitants of America. The arrival of European settlers had terrible consequences for the Indian tribes who were decimated by diseases previously unknown to them, and also massacred. Today, the remaining population live in reservations in Oklahoma, Arizona and New Mexico. Which of these headdresses are the same?

Solution: B and D

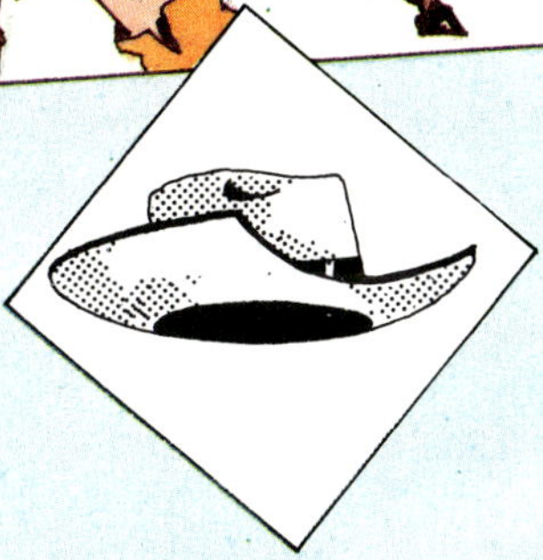

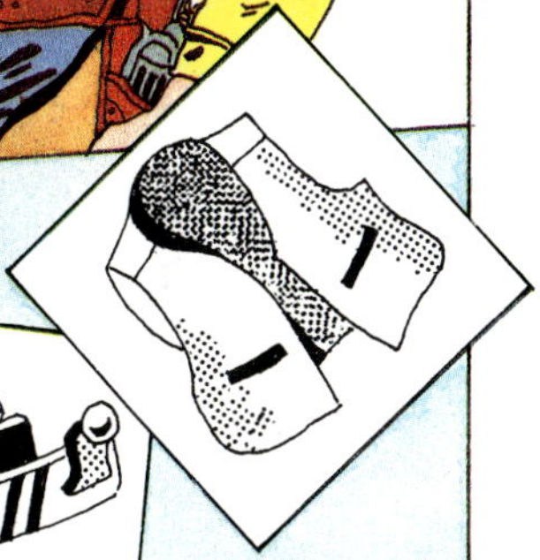

Cowboys look after the huge herds of cattle on the prairies of the West. Nowadays most cowboys work up north in Wyoming and Montana.

These cowboys here set off in a hurry and left a few things behind. Can you complete their outfits?

Solution: (From left to right) holster; chaps; spur; glove

Rubbing noses with the Eskimos

Alaska is in the north-west of the continent. The Arctic Circle cuts across this state so it has a polar climate: for many months it is covered by a thick blanket of ice and snow. Alaska is the biggest of the states, but it has the smallest population. It is the home of the Eskimos, the Aleutians and the Indians who live from hunting, fishing and tourism. Now the discovery of oil has changed the old ways.

All these animals except one live in Alaska.

Solution: Penguins live at the South Pole.

In winter, Eskimos wrap up in thick, fur-lined clothes. For transport they use sleighs or snow-mobiles.
When they go on a hunt, they camp out in igloos made from blocks of snow but normally they live in modern houses.

These Eskimo children have put on their traditional costume for a special occasion. Spot the 5 differences.

Rock around the clock!

Most modern music styles came from America: Country music, Blues, Jazz, Rock 'n' Roll . . .

The guitar is the star performer in all of these, but each type of music has its own type of guitar.
Find the right guitar for each player.

Solution: A2, B3, C1

American heroes

Rin Tin Tin's Cabin

The Last of Uncle Tom

Gone With the Mohicans

Davy Sawyer

Tom Crockett

The Wind and Huckleberry Finn

Meet some famous characters from American books and films. You'll certainly recognize most of them once you've untangled the titles of their stories which don't seem quite right . . .

Solution: Gone With the Wind; The Last of the Mohicans; Uncle Tom's Cabin; Tom Sawyer and Huckleberry Finn; Davy Crockett; Rin Tin Tin

Dreams come true in Hollywood – at least on the screen. You've seen the films, now gaze at the stars. Can you put a name to each of these silhouettes?

Solution: The Pink Panther; Donald Duck; Fred Astaire; Droopy; Popeye; Marilyn Monroe; Woody Woodpecker; Tweety Pie; Charlie Chaplin.

Made in the USA

You probably have a good deal in common with American kids:
You listen to the same music, you watch the same films and I'm sure you love hamburgers, popcorn and Coke!

Now look at all these images from American everyday life and unmask the intruders.

Solution: There is a Canadian Mountie, a Spanish stamp and an English coin.

Reach for the sky!

Skyscrapers make up the skyline of all major American cities, but they are usually occupied by offices. Most people live in individual houses.
Some of these skyscrapers are more than 100 storeys high . . . If you are not afraid of heights, find someone to do this colouring race with you. Throw the die in turns and colour in the storey which corresponds to the number on your die. The first to complete the paintwork wins the game.

Imprimerie-Offset-Aubin, Poitiers — Dépôt légal n° 355-3-1986 (P 13883)
Collection n° 24 — Edition n° 92 — 24/1142/9